WHEN I PRAY
VOLUME 2

WHEN I PRAY
VOLUME 2

31 More Days of Wisdom for Women
From the Book of Psalms

Kristy L. Marcotte

STFW Press

LEE'S SUMMIT, MISSOURI

Kristy L. Marcotte/STFW Press
196A NW Oldham Pkwy #105
Lee's Summit, MO 64081
www.KristyMarcotte.com

Book layout ©2014 BookDesignTemplates.com

When I Pray Volume 2 - 31 More Days of Wisdom for Women From the Book of Psalms / Kristy L. Marcotte -- 1st ed.
ISBN 978-0-9984079-4-4

Dedication

*I dedicate this book to my mom, Patricia Dunn
who is now in Heaven with Jesus.*

*I am eternally grateful that she pointed
me to Christ and provided a perfect example
of what it looked like to live a life powered
by passionate persistent prayer.
Love you Mom, see you soon.*

CONTENTS

INTRODUCTION

N EED WISDOM FOR when you're facing a road-block, finding rest in spite of overwhelm, or keeping prayer simple? Like the first When I Pray devotional; I've packed this book with another 31 days of devotions that will take you even deeper in your walk with God.

If you haven't read the first one, that's okay. But do plan to buy it when you're finished with this one.

Each devotion includes a verse from the Book of Psalms, a note from me, and a prayer to pray for each day of the month. I have intentionally designed this book to help you connect with God every day in spite of your busy schedule.

Besides a Bible and pen, you will want to have a journal to get the most out of this book. Don't have one? No worries. You can still start today by going to my website and downloading my free prayer journal pages. Here is the link: www.straighttalkforwomen.com/resources/when-i-pray-devotional/. After downloading the pages, print them and you're ready to go.

Remember, there is power when you pray. So, sit down, buckle up and get ready for God's power to ener-gize your prayer time over the next 31 days!

- Kristy Marcotte

DAY 1
WISDOM WHEN ASKING
FOR THE DESIRES OF MY HEART

"Take delight in the LORD,

and he will give you your heart's desires."

Psalm 37:4 (NLT)

WHAT ARE THE desires of your heart? What do you desire for your marriage? What do you desire for your career? What do you desire for your family?

Have you really thought about what your desires are? Did you even know that God wants you to take delight in Him and that He will give you the desires of your heart? It's important to note that He didn't say "be perfect" and I will give you your heart's desires. He said, "Take delight...", big difference.

The word delight means to take pleasure in something, so God is essentially saying, *take pleasure in me.* Think about one thing that you really enjoy doing. For me, I really enjoy going for a boat ride out on a lake. There is something so calming and relaxing about a really slow, leisurely boat ride. The feeling is hard to explain, but I could do that all day long.

God wants us to feel that way about Him. Would you enjoy spending the whole day with God just enjoying His presence? If you don't know the answer to that question, maybe you don't know Him that well. As much as I enjoy a leisurely boat ride out on a lake, even more, I would enjoy a day with God, praying and reading the Bible. I feel I grow so much and feel closer to Him the more I spend time with Him. The inner peace and insight I gain from spending time with God is so awesome.

You can have this same experience with God. He wants to spend time with you. He wants you to know Him so well that you truly take delight in Him. This week, work on spending a little extra time with Him. Pick one day and put it on the schedule to spend an extra hour. Just pray and read the Bible. Tell Him what your desires are for your relationships, your career, and your future. Build this habit into your weekly routine, and I guarantee over time you will start to see your heart's desires fulfilled.

Today's Prayer:

Lord, thank you for your promise in Psalm 37:4 that if I focus on delighting in you then you will give me the desires of my heart. Lord, one desire of my heart is (fill in the blank). I know the more time I spend with you the more I will delight in you. Please help me carve out time this next week to spend one extra hour talking to you and reading your Word. When that time comes, help me resist any distractions. In Jesus' name, I pray, AMEN.

DAY 2
WISDOM FOR TRUSTING GOD
WITH THE DETAILS

"Commit everything you do to the Lord.

Trust him, and he will help you."

Psalm 37:5 (NLT)

SEVERAL YEARS AGO, during Christmas time, I was out shopping and came across a beautiful, artificial Christmas tree. I had been wanting to get an artificial one to go in our formal living room area for a really long time but just couldn't get approval from my finance department, a.k.a. my hubby, to make the purchase. He didn't quite understand why we needed a second Christmas tree in the living room if we already had a real one in the family room.

When you come in the front door of our house, you can't see the Christmas tree that's in our family room, so that's why I wanted a second one for our living room. He, of course, thought I was being ridiculous and promptly forfeited my request to spend $350 dollars on an artificial one. So I decided to take this one up with my dad, a.k.a. my heavenly Father. I prayed He would help me find a reasonably priced artificial tree and that God would soften Brian's stone cold heart... um, I mean...Brian's heart, and let me get it. LOL!

Not long after, I was talking to my cousin about wanting an artificial tree and asked where she bought hers. To my surprise, she said I could have hers because she just bought a brand new one! Can you believe it?

Not only did I get a beautiful artificial tree to put in my formal living room, it was TOTALLY FREEEEE! Now that's how our God does it. Knowing how much He cared about the tiniest of details in my life helped me trust Him for the big stuff even more.

The next time you think God's probably too busy to ask Him for help with the little details, think again! Psalm 37:5 says to "*Commit everything you do to the Lord. Trust Him, and He will help you...*" **even with the little details!**

Today's Prayer:

Lord, thank you for reminding me to commit absolutely everything I do to you knowing that if I trust you, you will help me. Even if it is a silly little request, help me to go to you in prayer first. Then, help me to trust in you to help me as you promise in Psalm 37:5. In Jesus' name, I pray, AMEN.

DAY 3
WISDOM FOR WAITING
ON GOD TO ACT

"Be still in the presence of the Lord,

and wait patiently for him to act."

Psalm 37:7a (NLT)

ARE YOU A wiggle-worm like me? I have a really hard time sitting still. I've been known to take "multi-tasking" to a whole other level! Let's just say, patience isn't one of my strengths.

The other morning I was making a list of what I was going to do while getting my hair done at the salon. It's a two and a half hour long procedure. My hairstylist chuckled as he watched me walk in with my laptop in tow. Needless to say, I never opened it. LOL

During my hair appointment, I needed to just be still and wait patiently for my hairstylist to work his magic. I always know I'm going to love it when he's done but sitting still and waiting feels like forever. But I know that if we don't wait for the highlights to come up to the right shade of blonde, I'll end up with a not-so-desirable shade of orange. So, as much as I dislike the long wait, wait I will.

Just like at the hair salon, sometimes, we have to *be still* and *wait* patiently for God to act. But so often I feel compelled to do something to speed up the process while I'm waiting. Do you ever feel this way?

I want to help God get things going little faster. When I do this, I often get ahead of Him and end up with a not-so-desirable outcome. Sound familiar?

If you're tempted to push things along or even rush a head of God, like me, DON'T. Remember Psalm 37:7a and choose instead to be still and wait patiently for Him to act. Though it may seem like things are going slowly, God's timing is always perfect.

Today's Prayer:

Lord, I desperately need your help when I have to wait. I am struggling with waiting for (fill in the blank). Please give me the power to be still in your presence and wait patiently for you to act. I cannot do it by myself. I tend to run ahead of you to make things happen on my own. When I'm tempted to do this, please remind me of Psalm 37:7. In Jesus' name, I pray, AMEN.

DAY 4:
WISDOM FOR WHEN
CIRCUMSTANCES SEEM DISMAL

"O Lord my god, you have performed many wonders for us.

Your plans for us are too numerous to list.

You have no equal. If I tried to recite all your wonderful

deeds, I would never come to the end of them."

Psalm 40:5 (NLT)

MAYBE YOUR FIRST response to this verse is, I just can't think of anything to be thankful for right now. Well, then this is a really good day for you!

I have discovered that when my circumstances are down-right dismal, and I read a verse like this one, I need to sit down and force myself to think for a while about all the wonderful things God has done for me recently.

Soon, those dark dismal clouds begin to fade slightly. When I make the extra effort to actually write this list down on paper, the dark clouds fade even more and soon my whole perspective has done a 180 degree turn.

If your circumstances are looking down-right dismal, force yourself to write a list of everything God has done for you recently.

Write down even the silly little things like when your friend gives you a jean jacket right before you were planning to go buy one. Yes, that really happened to me and it was the exact style I wanted. Coincidence? Nope…God!

After writing down everything you can think of, say Psalm 40:5 out loud. Then say a prayer of thankfulness to God for each of the items on the list.

As you shift your focus from the dismal circumstance to the list of awesome things God has done, those dark clouds will soon disappear.

Today's Prayer:

Lord, thank you for Psalm 40:5. Lord, you have performed many wonders for us. Your plans for us are too numerous to list. You have no equal. If I tried to recite all your wonderful deeds, I would never come to the end of them. Here is a list of everything I can think of that I'm thankful for (fill in the blank). Please help me remember this list next time my circumstances look dismal. In Jesus' name, I pray, AMEN.

DAY 5
WISDOM FOR KNOWING
GOD IS PRESENT

> *"God is our refuge and strength,*
>
> *an ever-present help in times of trouble."*
>
> *Psalm 46:1(GW)*

D O YOU SOMETIMES get that feeling that you're in trouble? I do. I get it just about every week when something unexpected happens that I didn't plan for and I've foolishly over-packed my schedule.

How about you? How about when you're running late for work, jump into the car ready to zoom off and realize you're on vapors, and have to get gas? How about when you realize there are more bills than money to pay them, and you wonder... *God, where are you? Do you even see what's going on?*

Psalm 46:1 promises that He does. It says, *"God is our refuge and strength an ever-present help in times of trouble"*. God is "ever-present." Just think about that for a minute.

According to Webster's Dictionary, ever-present means "being present always." God is always present, with everyone. He sees all. He knows all. If this is hard for you to grasp, that's okay.

I don't completely understand how airplanes get up in the air weighing over a hundred thousand pounds and travel at like 550 miles per hour but that never stops me from booking a flight when I want to go on vacation.

Similar to my lack of understanding how airplanes fly, my lack of understanding how God does what He does has never stopped me from depending on Him for help. Don't let it stop you, either.

God is right beside you now. He knows every detail of what you're facing today. Don't you worry your little brain with the how part. All you need to remember is that He is your refuge and strength, an ever-present help no matter what trouble you're facing.

Today's Prayer:

Lord, thank you for Psalm 46:1. Thank you for reminding me that you are my refuge and strength an ever-present help in times of trouble. Right now I'm feeling overwhelmed with (fill in the blank). I believe you're with me, even if I don't understand how. Please help me to feel your presence when I start to feel alone or overwhelmed. In Jesus' name, I pray, AMEN.

DAY 6
WISDOM FOR WHEN
I'VE MESSED UP...AGAIN

"Have mercy on me, O' God, because of your

unfailing love. Because of your great compassion,

blot out the stain of my sins."

Psalm 51:1 NLT

I DON'T KNOW ABOUT you, but I have to pray this prayer to God...often, more often than I care to admit. It's such a relief that God's mercy is based on HIS unfailing love, not on anything I do.

You don't have to read through too many books of the Old Testament to get a glimpse of His amazingly great compassion either.

I can't believe how many times God saved the Israelites from imminent disaster, that they often brought on themselves. But He did, over and over again. I certainly would not have put up with their shenanigans as long as God did. Aren't you glad I'm not God? Me, too. ☺

When I'm in need of God's great compassion to blot out the stain of my sins... for the 10th time, I want that same great compassion He showed the Israelites, don't you?

When you start beating yourself up for messing up yet again, remember God's mercy based on His unfailing love and great compassion is available to you as often as you need it.

And, by the way, consider extending this same mercy to others. The devotion was sounding great until that last sentence, I know. But, I know you can do it. Just remember all the times God has given you mercy and it will be super easy to extend that same mercy to others.

Today's Prayer:

Lord, thank you for having mercy on me and blotting out the stain of my sins because of your unfailing love and great compassion. Lord, I admit that I keep failing at (fill in the blank). Please forgive me and help me change. Lord, when I am tempted to beat myself up, quickly remind me of Psalm 51:1. When others fail me, Lord, help me to extend mercy to them as you do to me. In Jesus' name, I pray, AMEN.

DAY 7
WISDOM FOR GETTING
A CLEAN SLATE

"Create in me a clean heart, O God.

Renew a loyal spirit within me."

Psalm 51:10 (NLT)

I DON'T KNOW ABOUT you, but the older I get the more I realize just how "human" I really am. I could probably use a good slate cleaning oh say at the end of every day.

Psalm 51:10 is David's prayer to God after he sinned by committing adultery with Bathsheba.

This verse is a perfect for helping us remember who's doing the cleaning and renewing. Guess what, it's not us. It's our loving heavenly Father who can create a clean heart and renew a loyal spirit within us. Our job is to do the asking. Now that's good news, right?

I'm so glad it's not up to me to do the cleaning because I know my track record, and it's not very good. I desperately need a loving God to help me do for myself what I know I cannot do on my own.

Oh, I've tried, but like I said before, the older I get, the more I realize I just can't fix myself. I hate to be the bearer of bad news, but, neither can you.

We read in Psalm 103:14 (NLT), *"For he [God] knows how weak we are; he remembers we are only dust."*

What problem are you pretending isn't really a problem? Give up. We don't need to pretend with God because He knows how weak we are. In Psalm 51:10, David provides a perfect example of a prayer we can pray to God every day.

So, if you're in desperate need of a clean slate, pray this verse to God today, just like David did.

Today's Prayer:

Lord, thank you for Psalm 51:10. I am so glad that I can come to you when I've blown it and need a clean slate. Thank you for reminding me that you're the one who does the cleaning and renewing, and it's my job to do the asking. This morning I ask you to create in me a clean heart and renew a loyal spirit within me. Thank you for knowing how human I really am and still loving me. When my loyalty runs thin, or I blow it again, bring this verse to my mind, so I will remember to run to you immediately instead of trying to fix my life on my own. In Jesus' name, I pray, AMEN.

DAY 8
WISDOM FOR RESPONDING TO CRITICISM

"Come with great power, O God, and rescue me!

Defend me with your might."

Psalm 54:1 (NLT)

DO YOU EVER feel like you're always defending yourself?

Sometimes, we shouldn't jump to defend ourselves so quickly. Don't take this statement the wrong way. I'm not saying to be a doormat at all, but sometimes when we're criticized it's best to remain silent and let our heavenly Father "Come with great power, rescue us, and defend us with HIS might".

Three things to consider before jumping to defend yourself:

1. Consider the source:

Who is criticizing you? Are they someone who demonstrates great wisdom in the area where you are being criticized? If the answer is no, consider remaining silent and rely on God to come to your defense.

2. Consider the reason behind the specific criticism:

Is what they are saying driven by well thought-out logic? Again, if the answer is no, consider remaining silent. If they are reacting to a situation "in the heat" of the moment based on emotions, it is unlikely that you will be able to talk them out of it using logic.

3. Consider remaining silent even if the answer is "yes" to the first two considerations:

Why? Because it's always better to accept the criticism quietly first and then go to God and pray Psalm 54:1. Ask Him if it is truly necessary for you to respond or not.

Maybe you do still need to respond, but you will have sought God's wisdom and guidance first. I get myself into trouble so often because I want to pounce the second I'm criticized for something. Then afterwards, I almost always regret what's come out of my mouth.

If you can relate, pray Psalm 54:1 along with me this morning.

Today's Prayer:

Lord, I know you saw that I was criticized for (fill in the blank). I pray you will come with great power, rescue me, and defend me with your might! Give me the wisdom to know whether I need to respond or if I should remain silent. The next time I receive criticism, help me to keep from jumping to my own defense and, instead, go to you first in prayer. In Jesus' name, I pray, AMEN!

Day 9
Wisdom for How
to Complain

"As for me, I will call on God, and the Lord will save me.

Evening, and morning, and at noon,

I will make my complaint and murmur

and He will hear my voice."

Psalms 55:16-17 (MEV)

D O YOU EVER feel guilty for complaining? I do. I try not to complain because I know Philippians 2:14-15 (NLT) tells us to…

"Do everything without complaining and arguing, so that no one can criticize you. Live clean, innocent lives as children of God, shining like bright lights in a world full of crooked and perverse people."

Let's look closer at what these verses are really saying. Are you ready? This is so cool! Though both Psalms 55:16-17 and Philippians 2:14-15 seem like they are saying the same thing, but they aren't at all.

Philippians 2:15 says that we should do everything

without complaining so that no one can criticize us, meaning that we shouldn't be complaining in front of others.

On the contrary, Psalms 55:16-17 is describing David talking to God directly. Verse 17 says *"...I will make my complaint and murmur and He [God] will hear my voice."*

Because we can talk to God without even opening our mouths, we can follow David's example and complain to our heart's content!

It's not like God doesn't already know how you feel anyway. Because He already knows your thoughts, He's not going to be surprised when you start venting about something that's really bugging you.

Whether you speak to Him in your mind (you introverts) or you go into your bedroom, shut the door, turn up the TV so no one can hear, and let it out *aloud* (us extroverts), God can handle your complaints.

I've done this several times, usually when no one is home, of course. I love that I can be real with God! And you can too!

Later today, when you're tempted to complain to your friend about something, take your complaint to God instead. Don't get me wrong; you need one or two people in your life that you can share anything with. But keep your complaints between you and God.

Start right now. Just me talking about complaining probably got you thinking about that "thing" someone did that just really ticked you off. Now that I brought up the topic, why don't you talk to God about it right now.

Go ahead… complain away! God can handle whatever you have to say.

Today's Prayer:

Lord, I'm really ticked off that (fill in the blank). Thank you for your promise in Psalms 55:16–17 that no matter if it's in the evening, in the morning or at noon, I can come to you with my complaints and you will hear my voice. Thank you that it doesn't matter what I say, you can handle it. When I'm tempted to complaining to someone, remind me to go to you instead. In Jesus' name, I pray, AMEN.

DAY 10
WISDOM TO SEE GOD'S
PROTECTION

"Because you are my helper, I sing for joy

in the shadow of your wings."

Psalm 63:7 (NLT)

D O YOU FEEL like singing for joy today? No? Some days, neither do I. But when I came to this verse, something just made me read it a few more times.

David, the author of this Psalm was often facing life or death situations. But because we don't normally face these kinds of situations, I struggled to relate to his "sing for joy" moment...until the other night.

While on my way home, I sat in my car in the left turn lane of an intersection waiting for my light to turn green. The green light lit up and I began to enter the intersection. As I curved to the left, I looked to the right and noticed a car approaching the intersection at high speed. Everything seemed to slow down as I tried to determine whether or not he was going to stop for the red light.

In that split second, my brain- *probably God* - provided the right answer. I slammed on the brakes as he flew by at what had to be at least 60+ miles per hour!

I sat in the middle of the intersection –frozen. *Did that just really happen*, I thought. Very gingerly, my right foot re-engaged with the gas pedal and I crawled through the intersection.

As I continued at a snail's pace down the street, tears began to roll down my cheeks overwhelmingly grateful for God's obvious physical protection. The rest of the drive home was one continuously looping "sing for joy" moment!

We often think that life-threatening situations are rare. Are they? I bet there's numerous times when God protected me and my family from harm, but we just never realized it.

The same is probably true for you. Just because you don't see God protecting you, doesn't mean He isn't. As you go about your day, think about how God might be protecting you and your family from harm. Let that thought fill your heart with gratefulness.

Because God is your helper, sing for joy in the shadow of His wings –TODAY!

Today's Prayer:

Lord, because you are my helper, whether I see you or not, I will sing for joy in the shadow of your wings. When I start to become complacent or feel alone in my circumstances; remind me that you're near and still protecting me. In Jesus' name, I pray, AMEN.

DAY 11
WISDOM FOR
OVERCOMING DOUBT

*"You faithfully answer our prayers with your awesome deeds,
O God, our Savior..."*

Psalm 65:5a (NLT)

LIKE THE VERSE in yesterday's devotion, this Psalm was written by David as well. He was clearly speaking from experience that built a foundation of faith and trust that God would faithfully answer his prayers.

Do you have this kind of faith? Sometimes I do, and sometimes, I don't. When I start doubting God will answer my prayers, it's usually a telltale sign I'm spending less time with Him.

If I'm not careful to spend time with Him every day, I quickly become overwhelmed by doubt. The more time I spend wallowing in my problems, the bigger they become. The more time I spend with God, the bigger He becomes, and the smaller the problems become.

If you're feeling overwhelmed by doubt, here are four steps to take:

1. List all the things God has done for you recently.

This list will help you remember that He will help you now just as He has in the past. Include everything you can think of, big and small.

2. Carve out the first hour of your day and spend it reading the Bible.

There is power in God's Word. It is not the same as reading a self-help book. They can offer good advice, but no book has the power to change your mind or your heart more than the Word of God! When you come across a verse that speaks to you, write it down and meditate on it for several days.

3. Spend time talking to God about the circumstance that has your stomach in knots.

Write down what your specific request is regarding the issue and talk to Him about it. Tell Him how you feel and ask the tough questions. He can handle hearing them. Don't forget to sit in silence and wait for Him to answer. DO NOT SKIP this step!

4. Reach out to someone and ask for them to pray for you.

We need each other. Text a friend and tell them you are struggling. And, yes, be open and honest about what the issue is. Don't be vague.

Quit trying to pretend you have it all together. Everyone already knows you don't. Not only will you receive more prayer, but you will gain a deeper friendship. We all could use deeper friendships, *amen?*

When you are overcome with doubt, take the four steps I shared and you WILL believe... *"God will faithfully answer your prayers with His awesome deeds."*

Today's Prayer:

Lord, thank you for reminding me that you will faithfully answer my prayers with your awesome deeds. I'm specifically thankful for (fill in the blank). Help me to carve out time every day to spend with you. I know doing this will help shrink my doubts and increase my faith. In Jesus' name, I pray, AMEN.

DAY 12
WISDOM FOR
DEFEATING DISCOURAGEMENT

"O Lord, I have come to you for protection;

don't let me be disgraced. Save me and rescue me,

for you do what is right. Turn your ear to

listen to me, and set me free."

Psalms 71:1-2 (NLT)

HAVE YOU EVER felt so discouraged that you can't see any light at the end of the tunnel? If this thought describes you this morning, make Psalms 71:1-2 your prayer to today.

I have been friends with God for over three decades now, and I know He will protect me. He has bailed me out so many times, I really have no good reason ever to feel discouraged. However, I am also very human, unfortunately. ☺

I can end my morning prayer time with God all pumped up and ready to take on the world, and two hours later, feel overwhelming discouragement.

Yep. I know. This isn't what you would expect to hear from someone who's supposed to be "encouraging and full of faith" blah, blah, blah... Well, I hate to break the bad news but that's just not me.

Just because I'm the one writing this devotional book doesn't mean I've somehow risen above feeling discouraged. I struggle just like you.

It's okay to be discouraged. Just, DON'T LET IT DEFEAT YOU! Reading and meditating on encouraging verses in God's Word is how I defeat discouragement.

This reason is precisely why I love reading the Psalms and have shared many of them with you. God's Word is the unexplainable unending, unfailing power you need to defeat discouragement. Start with praying Psalms 71:1-2 today.

Today's Prayer:

"Lord, I come to you this morning. I need your protection right now. I am feeling really discouraged with (fill in the blank) and pray that you will not let me be disgraced. Please, save me and rescue me, for I know that you do what is right. I pray this morning that you will turn your ear to listen to me, and set me free!" In Jesus' name, I pray, AMEN.

DAY 13
WISDOM FOR
INCREASING STRENGTH

"Whom have I in heaven but you?

I desire you more than anything on earth.

My health may fail,

and my spirit may grow weak,

but God remains the strength of my heart;

he is mine forever."

Psalms 73:25-26 (NLT)

THIS IS SO my morning motto --*NOT!* I would love for Psalms 73: 25-26 to be my heartfelt feeling first thing in the morning when I start my prayer time. Who wouldn't, right?

But in reality, it just isn't so. It's more like: "Hey Lord, thank you for helping me yesterday... Okay, so for today, please, I need you to..., help me to..., and give me strength for..."

Does this list of requests sound remotely familiar to what your morning prayer time sounds like?

At first glance, Psalms 73:25-26 seemed a little bit far-fetched, but there was something about theses verses that I really wanted to be true for me. Maybe you feel the same?

When I get this feeling while reading a set of verses, I treat it like a sign that I should take some time to meditate on them a little longer.

One way to meditate on scripture is to read the verses over and over again. So, let's do that now. Take a moment to read over the two verses several times. Read them in your mind a couple of times and then read them out loud a few times.

Think about it- whom else do we have in heaven? No one. It is true that we should desire Him more than anything on earth, even our families. Frankly, God is the only one who can give us the strength we need to love our family members unconditionally.

I don't know about you, but my health certainly isn't what it used to be. I have to work twice as hard to feel half as good as I used to.

What is so powerful is that the verses don't end there. They end with *"God remains the strength of my heart, he is mine forever!"* That is an awesome promise from our awesome God!

The more you meditate on that part, the more your heart's desire for God above all else in your life grows! Starting to get the idea?

Look what God promises us in Luke 8:18 (NLT); *"So pay attention to how you hear, to those who listen to my teaching, more understanding will be given..."* The more you meditate on God's Word, the more understanding you will have.

What kind of strength do you need today? Do you need more physical strength? Need more emotional strength? Need more spiritual strength? The secret…*feed on God's Word daily.*

Today's Prayer:

Lord, Thank you for Psalms 73:25-26. It is true, whom have I in heaven but you? I desire you more than anything on earth. My health may fail, and my spirit may grow weak, but you, Lord, will remain the strength of my heart. You are mine forever." When I begin to feel weak emotionally, physically, or spiritually, remind me to feed on your Word. In Jesus' name, I pray, AMEN.

DAY 14
WISDOM FOR
FACING A ROADBLOCK

"Your road led through the sea,

your pathway through the mighty waters –

a pathway no one knew was there!"

Psalm 77:19 (NLT)

FACING A MAJOR roadblock? Maybe you've been working really hard at something and once again you've suffered a major setback. Perhaps you're beginning to wonder if you should just give up and quit.

Or maybe you've even had this thought; I must be fighting against God himself! Have you ever felt like God was playing a cruel joke on you? Have you ever asked Him, *What kind of game are you playing.... Help me out here!*

I promise, you're not alone. I have thought it all - and then some.

Can you imagine for just a minute what the Israelites must have been thinking when God led them out of slavery from Egypt? They must have been so elated!

If this deliverance happened today, they would be texting all their friends, sending snapchats, taking selfies with Moses and Aaron, and of course they would have to do a big group selfie with the outline of all the Egyptian pyramids in the background.

However, by the next day, all the awesomeness of the miracle God did the day before has now worn off. All the kids are asking Moses, *"When are we gonna get there?"* No one cares about their sore feet. They're too busy freaking out there's no more free WiFi, their cell phone batteries are all dying, and not to mention - everyone is starving.

Suddenly, someone looks up ahead and spots the Red Sea off in the distance. I would imagine that by now, they are all feeling pretty "Hangry".

By the way, if you don't know what "hangry" is, it means you're both *hungry* and *angry* at the same time. If this is the first time you've heard this word, it just means you don't have a teenager around to keep you up on the cool new words everyone is using. LOL

Are you facing a Red Sea today and feeling a little *"hangry"*?

Last week, I made several plans to work on some major projects. Well, let's just say; the week started with a nail in my tire and ended with a trip to the hospital emergency room.

You could say I was feeling just a little hangry by the end of the week and wondering if maybe I should just give up.

What Red Sea are you facing this week? Is it a Red Sea in your career? Is it a Red Sea in a relationship? Is it a

Red Sea in your health? Is it a Red Sea in your finances? It says in Psalm 77:19, *"Your road led through the sea, your pathway through the mighty waters --a pathway no one knew was there!"*

Our God is a God who can make a pathway right straight through the seas that you're facing! He doesn't need bridges, boats, or airplanes!

Sometimes, God wants to use a pathway you didn't know was there.

Today's Prayer:

Lord, thank you for Psalm 77:19 reminding me that your road may lead right straight through the sea in my life. Your pathway may take me straight through the mighty waters, a pathway no one new was even there. I'm facing a Red Sea of (fill in the blank). Lord, I'm going to depend on you to provide a pathway through it. I can't see it right now, but I trust you're going to get me through. In Jesus' name, I pray, AMEN.

DAY 15
WISDOM WHEN WEIGHED
DOWN BY "SHOULD-DOS"

"For he remembered that they were merely mortal,

gone like a breath of wind that never returns."

Psalm 78:39 (NLT)

DO YOU OFTEN feel this heavy cloud of "should-dos" hovering over you? Every day the cloud seems to hover lower and lower until it feels more like a heavy weight on your shoulders than a cloud.

When I don't do all of my "should-dos", I feel an incredible amount of guilt. Then my sick sense of optimism compels me to add them all to the next day. Because of course, I will have more time tomorrow, right? Not.

If we're not careful, this kind of thinking can keep us feeling imprisoned and guilt-ridden day after day. Psalm 78:39 helps us remember that yes, we are in fact mortal. It's funny that we need to be reminded of this condition.

I don't know about you, but I need to be reminded all the time. Every time I discover some cool new app or learn some new productivity tip, somehow I think I will be able to complete twice as much as before.

Here's a little secret that will blow your mind…God chose you! Even though you and I are mere mortals with huge limitations, God chose us! According to John 15:19 (NIV), *"…you do not belong to the world, but I have chosen you out of the world…"*

Write this statement in your journal…I am only human, yet I was still chosen by God! The next time you start to berate yourself for not finishing something you started (my specialty) or feel weighed down by a long list of "should-dos," remind yourself that you are in fact HUMAN and chosen by a God who knows how mortal you are and still chose you.

Today's Prayer:

Lord, thank you for understanding that we are only human. I sometimes feel so weighed down by a never ending list of "should-dos". Help me to remember that you chose me in spite of my humanness, and I am so grateful that you did! Help me to remember Psalm 78:39 when I am tempted to add even more onto my plate. In Jesus' name, I pray, AMEN.

Day 16
Wisdom for Going
Through a Valley

"When they walk through the valley of weeping,

it will become a place of refreshing springs.

The autumn rains will clothe it with blessings."

Psalm 84:6 (NIV)

Are you in a valley of weeping today? You're not alone. This verse reminds us that it's not *if*, it's *when* they walk through the valley of weeping.

Everyone walks through these valleys in life. But God promises they will become a place of refreshing springs and the autumn rains will clothe them with blessings.

Here are three things you can do while you're in the valley of weeping that will help along the way.

1. Realize it's okay to feel sadness and cry when you're going through a valley.

It's not called the "valley of weeping" for nothing. Don't feel like you have to pretend everything is fine when it isn't. Many times, while talking to God, my prayers have turned into crying to Him.

I often feel better after I've had a good crying session with God. He often opens my eyes to see things I couldn't see before.

It's completely okay to be real with God. When you're scared or angry or hopeless about a situation, tell God. He can handle it.

2. Reach out and share what you're going through with a close friend.

Choose a Christian friend who's a good listener. Choose someone who won't minimize the situation, will be encouraging, and will pray for you. It's often hard to even know what to pray when you're really in a deep valley.

3. Find a special Bible verse that encourages you and memorize it.

Write Psalm 84:6 or whatever verse encourages you everywhere. Put it on your cell phone as the background. Put it on your laptop as a background image.

Write the verse on a 3x5 index card and keep it in your purse. Write it on a second index card and clip it on your car visor so every time you get in, you will see it.

Every time you get out your journal, write the special verse at the top of each page every day while you're going through the valley. Write it as a prayer to God. Every time you start to feel sad or think about the situation, read the verse out loud over and over. I don't care if this idea sounds a little kooky, just do it!

I have grown much closer to God while going through valleys than any other time in my life. Reminding myself of this truth has become a refreshing spring clothed with blessings that keep overflowing in my life again and again.

I don't know how God does it, but He just does. And, He will do the same for you. I guess that is why He is God, and we're not, right?

In your life there will be valleys of weeping, but God can use them for good. He can bring about a refreshing spring from all of your tears.

Today's Prayer:

Lord, this morning I come to you with (fill in the blank). I know you're going to help me get through it because Psalm 84:6 says when we walk through the valley of weeping, it will become a place of refreshing springs. The autumn rains will clothe it with blessings, but I'm still in the middle and struggling. Help me feel you are close and give me peace knowing you'll get me through this valley somehow. In Jesus' name, I pray, AMEN.

DAY 17
WISDOM FOR KNOWING
GOD'S GOOD THINGS

"For the Lord God is our sun and our shield.

He gives us grace and glory. The Lord will withhold

no good thing from those who do what is right."

Psalm 84:11 (NLT)

G OD HAS GOOD things for you.
Woohoo! Now, this is my kind of verse! It has it all!

When I first read Psalm 84:11, I loved it so much that I re-wrote the verse in my journal. I often write a verse that sticks out to me in my journal to reflect on it more.

Below the verse I wrote a list of things that I felt were "good things". You know, things like doubling sales in my business next month or getting a really good deal on a new pair of shoes I've been wanting. Then I heard…

God: *Those are good things in **your** eyes.*

Me: *So, what are good things in your eyes, Lord?*

God: *Getting on a budget and slowing down to focus on planning instead of always looking for shortcuts*

Then, these two verses from Proverbs came to my mind:

"Know the state of your flocks, and put your heart into caring for your herds, for riches don't last forever."

Proverbs 27:23-24a (NLT)

"Good planning and hard work lead to prosperity, but hasty shortcuts lead to poverty."

Proverbs 21:5 (NLT)

Don't get me wrong; there is nothing wrong with the good things on my list. And they are still on my list, but God's "good things" don't often make it to the top of my list.

God, however, clearly wanted to make sure I remembered them. So much so that He reminded me of the verses in Proverbs. You know, just for back-up.

Now, it's your turn. Write Psalm 84:11 in your journal. Then make a list of all the "good things" you can think of.

Now, write this sentence to God: *This is my list of good things, Lord; what is yours?*

Sit quietly in God's presence. Let Him fill your mind with His list. Then begin writing things down that come to your mind. Remember, it's your journal. It's only for you and God.

Today's Prayer:

Lord, thank you for Psalm 84:11 that promises you will withhold no good thing from those who do what is right.

Lord, you know my heart and that I do strive to do what is right. In addition to the good things I've asked for like (fill in the blank), thank you for showing me the things you would like for me like (fill in the blank). Help me to always desire what is good in your eyes Lord. In Jesus' name, I pray, AMEN.

DAY 18
WISDOM FOR
KEEPING PRAYER SIMPLE

"Bend down, O Lord, and hear my prayer;

answer me, for I need your help."

Psalm 86:1 (NLT)

S O MANY THINGS in our lives are complicated. Sometimes, we can make things way more complicated than they need to be. Do you agree? Sometimes, we can even make things so complicated that we just don't feel like doing them anymore.

Do you ever feel this way about prayer? Have you ever wondered why we need to pray when God knows everything we need already? Think about it. He knows everything so that must include everything we need and want too, right?

It's not that we need to pray to Him so that He knows what we want; instead, our prayers show we are acknowledging two important truths. When we pray to God, we're acknowledging that we actually need help and that we believe God is the one who can help us.

While these truths help us understand the importance of prayer, there's no need to complicate the act of praying. Psalm 86:1 is a prayer that David prayed and a perfect example of how to keep prayer simple and to the point.

You don't need a bunch of flowery poetic paragraphs. Just sit quietly and pray this Psalm in your heart. Be real with God. Write down this verse in your journal.

If you want to get more specific, write the word "with…" after the verse and then list what you need help with.

Whatever it is, write it down. That situation, relationship, or problem you can't stop thinking about…write it down. Release it. Get it out of your mind and into God's hands.

God doesn't care if you use all the right words in your prayers. He cares that you've acknowledged your need for help and you've chosen to talk to Him about it.

Today's Prayer:

Lord, thank you for reminding me that I don't need to complicate my prayer time. I know you are so much bigger than me and my problems. I pray Psalm 86:1, bend down and hear my prayer, answer me because I need your help with (fill in the blank). In Jesus' name, I pray, AMEN.

DAY 19
WISDOM FOR
WHEN I NEED PROTECTION

"Protect me, for I am devoted to you.

Save me, for I serve you and trust you.

You are my God."

Psalm 86:2 (NLT)

S O OFTEN WE are let down by others that we stop relying on anyone. Many of our well-meaning friends and family make promises, then their lives get busy. It's nothing malicious or intentional, just life, being life.

Listen, GOD is NOT a person who gets too busy! He doesn't get overwhelmed by His own life. He doesn't have the limitations of time and space that we have.

In Psalm 86:2, David spoke to God as if He was "his very own God". We need to have this same perspective. Don't think of Him as "our" God, as in everyone's God, but think on a more personal level. Because He is God… not human, He can be *your God*, as much as He is mine or David's!

So – *your God* will never let you down. He is the one you should be depending on for protection! He never meant for you to be solely dependent upon other humans to meet all your needs, and He certainly didn't intend for you to solely depend upon your little old self to meet all your needs either.

What do you need protection from today? Get out your journal and start your list. Maybe you need protection from anything that would threaten to keep you from doing God's will. That was the first thing on my list. Maybe you need protection from self-doubt or the fear of failure.

What do you need to be saved from? Do you need to ask God to save you from yourself? I've prayed this many times. I'm my own worst enemy sometimes. Whatever it is you need protection from or saved from, ask. After-all, He is YOUR GOD!

Today's Prayer:

Lord, thank you for reminding me that you are my God and that I need to depend on you for my protection! I am devoted to you. Please protect me from (fill in your list). Save me, from (fill in the blank), for I serve you and trust you. You are my God! In Jesus' name, I pray, AMEN.

DAY 20
WISDOM FOR
CALLING ON GOD CONSTANTLY

"Be merciful to me O Lord,

For I am calling on you constantly."

Psalm 86:3 (NLT)

E VER FEEL LIKE God gets tired of hearing from you constantly?

I don't know about you but I am certainly calling on God constantly. Do you ever feel like sometimes He starts to get tired of hearing the same prayer for help over and over and over? I do.

When my girls were young and would come to me with repeated requests, after a while, my patience ran thin. At about the fifth request, instead of getting mom, they were greeted with what looked and sounded more like "Mom-zilla."

I know, totally unlike any other mom's reaction, right? LOL

When we constantly call on God for help, if we're not

careful, sometimes, we can picture Him reacting to us the same way that I reacted to my girls' repeated requests.

This thought couldn't be further from the truth!

Do not confuse your heavenly Father with your earthly father or mother. Doing so is a big mistake. God is never too busy for our constant requests. He doesn't get irritated when we ask for His help with the same thing over and over. He has all the time in the world for us. Being God has its perks, after all.

So, as you pray this morning, do not fear praying for the same thing for the tenth time-this week. It is totally okay for us to call on our heavenly Father constantly. He knows we are human and loves when we show our great dependence on Him – *yes, constantly!*

Today's Prayer:

"Lord, thank you so much for being merciful when I call on you constantly. Help me to remember that you want to hear from me every day, and calling on you constantly even for the same thing is totally fine with you. So, I'm going to ask once again for your help with - (fill in the blank). I'm going to keep coming to you every day with my many requests knowing that you won't resent or reject my asking. In Jesus' name, I pray, AMEN.

DAY 21
WISDOM WHEN ASKING
FOR HAPPINESS

"Give me happiness O Lord, for I give myself to you."

Psalm 86:4 (NLT)

I S IT JUST me, or would you agree that in some Christian circles the thought of asking God for happiness has gotten a bad rap. Somehow, we have been taught not to ask God to give us anything that will make us happy. You know, it's all about "Joy" and being "joyous in all circumstances". blah, blah, blah…

In Psalm 86:4, David is clearly asking God to give him happiness. Not sure there is any other way to interpret that verse. So, if David is okay with asking for happiness, then why can't we also be okay with it?

The second part of the verse also clearly shows David's heart when he said *"…for I give myself to you."* I think it is totally acceptable for us to ask for God to give us happiness if we've given Him our whole self.

God knows our hearts. He created us, so He knows when our motives are pure and when they aren't. He knows when we're asking for something that is just to make our lives easier but not necessarily better. He knows when we are asking for something good, but He wants to give us something better.

How's your heart this morning? Can you honestly say that you've given your whole self to Him? I can. You know why? Because I know He accepts me just the way I am, warts and all.

The same goes for you. He doesn't expect us to get our act together first. Get it? When we give ourselves to God, we can give Him all of us, even the broken parts.

If you know David, who wrote Psalm 86, you know his past. His selfish, sinful desires got another man's wife pregnant and then had him killed to cover it up. I love the fact that David was so real. He was a real person with real struggles, yet God loved him…all of him.

So, you can be sure that God will accept all of you as well. I challenge you to give your whole self to God today and don't be afraid to ask for happiness, too. This morning, write in your journal what your whole self looks like. Just write it all down, the good, the bad, and the ugly.

Then spend a few minutes writing down what happiness looks like to you. Write down everything that you can think of that defines happiness in your family, your work, and your future. Be specific.

The truth is that only when you fully give your whole self over to God can you truly be happy.

Today's Prayer:

Lord, I thank you for Psalm 86:4. Like David, I pray that you will give me happiness, for I give myself to you. Happiness for me is (fill in the blank). If out of everything I've asked for, you have something better in mind that you know will make me happier, I want that instead.

Thank you so much for loving and accepting me, even the not so good parts. I give all of myself to you including (fill in the blank). If there is anything that I have missed, show me so I can give 100% of myself over to you. I know that only when I have given my whole self over to you can I be truly happy! In Jesus' name, I pray, AMEN.

DAY 22
WISDOM WHEN
FEELING UNWORTHY

"O Lord, you are so good, so ready to forgive,

so full of unfailing love, for all who ask for your help."

Psalm 86:5 (NLT)

A T FIRST GLANCE you might skim over Psalm 86:5 quickly and miss the powerful nugget of truth in this verse. Sorry, can't let you do that today.

You might be wondering, *there are so many verses like this one, what is the 'nugget' I might miss?* When I first read this verse, I skimmed over it quickly and went right on to the next verse without much thought. But since I am writing a devotional book, I have been rereading verses over and over...for obvious reasons. LOL

Here's what I discovered. The more you read and reread God's Word, the more nuggets of truth you'll uncover in each verse.

What grabbed my attention about Psalm 86:5 was the word "ALL". This word is used so much in our everyday conversation that it has lost its pizazz. *Not today, girl-friend.*

God wants you to realize He is so ready to forgive, so full of unfailing love for ALL who ask for His help, not just the perfect or popular. His unfailing love is for us "*unworthys*" too.

Never let feeling unworthy keep you from asking for God's help. This verse is an awesome promise to cling to when you're feeling unworthy of God's love.

One important thing to remember is that our job is to do the asking. It's easy to shy away from asking for God's help when we've messed up for the 20th time. We think He's going to be shaking his head in disappointment. He's not.

Write down Psalm 86:5 in your journal and then list anything that makes you feel unworthy of God's help. During your prayer time, like David, thank God for His goodness, forgiveness, and unfailing love for you. Finally, take your requests to Him in prayer, knowing He is ready and waiting to help you.

Today's Prayer:

Lord, you are so good, so ready to forgive, so full of unfailing love, for all who ask for your help. Thank you for your unfailing love and forgiveness. This morning, I ask for your help with (fill in the blank). When I'm tempted to feel unworthy, remind me of Psalm 86:5. In Jesus' name, I pray, AMEN.

DAY 23
WISDOM FOR
ACTING ON GOD'S ANSWERS

"Listen closely to my prayer, O' Lord. Hear my urgent cry.

I will call to you whenever I'm in trouble

and you will answer me."

Psalms 86:6-7 (NLT)

FACING A BIG decision and unsure what to do? Maybe a crisis has just hit and you're facing enormous uncertainty. Or, perhaps you're stuck in a dead end job and desperately want out but don't know what to do about it.

Psalms 86:6-7 promises that whenever you call on God, He WILL answer. The question is will you act on that answer?

I admit, I have urgent prayer requests all the time. To me, everything is urgent, mainly because I tend to procrastinate. But that is a whole other devotion for another day.

I don't struggle so much believing God will answer but trusting the answer I'm hearing is really from God and not just my own idea, and then taking action. Do you ever have this struggle?

I go to God with my urgent need, He tells me what to do, and then I get cold feet and don't do anything. Have you ever done this?

So many times in the Old Testament of the Bible, God told someone to do something and promised to help them, but they had to make the first move. Like Noah with the ark. God told him to build an ark, but Noah had to start before there were any signs of rain.

Today, if you're in need of an answer from God, pray Psalms 86:6-7. If you're unsure if what you're hearing is really from God, enlist a close friend to pray with you for confirmation.

Once you're certain of God's answer, act on it. Don't delay. If you struggle with taking action like me, ask that same friend who prayed with you to hold you accountable.

Today's Prayer:

Lord, you promise in Psalms 86:6-7 that you will listen closely to my prayer. I come to you urgently for help with (fill in the blank). Thank you for promising that whenever I am in trouble and call on you, you will answer. Help me to hear your voice loud and clear. Then, help me to resist the temptation to delay taking action. In Jesus' name, I pray, AMEN.

DAY 24
WISDOM FOR WHEN
MY HOPE METER IS ON EMPTY

"Send me a sign of your favor.

Then those who hate me will be put to shame,

for you, O Lord, help and comfort me."

Psalm 86:17 (NLT)

HOW'S YOUR HOPE meter running this morning? Is it on empty? Feeling mounting pressure from all around to give up? I like that David, the author of Psalm 86, is straightforward. I love that he didn't beat around the bush in his prayers to God. Neither should we.

When I read this verse, I was going through a time of desperation. I was desperate for God to send me some sort of sign that I was on the right path. I had been praying and praying and doing and doing and yet I couldn't see any results. Have you ever felt this way?

Do you feel this way right now? Maybe you've been praying and waiting for God to do something in a relationship, and you're desperate for a sign of favor from Him.

Maybe you've been praying for a loved one to come to Christ, or perhaps, you've been praying for a loved one to turn back to Christ, and your hope meter is running low.

Maybe you've worked hard at your job and have been praying for a promotion, but it has yet to happen. Or maybe you've been working on launching your very own business and believe this is God's will, yet you're still spending more money than you're making, and there's pressure from all around to give up.

God wants more than anything for you to run to Him when you need help or comfort. So, if you're feeling overwhelming pressure to give up on something, no matter what it is, DON'T! Instead, boldly go to God this morning and pray Psalm 86:17.

Today's Prayer:

Lord, I boldly come and ask for you to send me a sign of your favor. Then those who hate me will be put to shame. For you, O Lord, help and comfort me. I need to know you hear me. Please show me a sign, so I know I'm on the right track. And if I'm not, show me that too. I want to do your will, Lord. I am feeling mounting pressure to give up on (fill in the blank). I desperately need a sign of your favor because I'm feeling very hopeless right now. I ask for your help and comfort today. In Jesus' name, I pray, AMEN.

DAY 25
WISDOM WHEN ASKING
FOR SUCCESS

"And may the Lord our God show us his approval

and make our efforts successful.

Yes, make our efforts successful!"

Psalm 90:17 (NLT)

D O YOU EVER pray for success? Sometimes, we feel guilty for wanting success because we think of it as being selfish or materialistic.

God wants us to be successful. If your success will help others, then you should be praying for God's help to make your efforts successful. What's the alternative, pray for failure? Now, that would be dumb.

I want to point out that the psalmist is asking for God to *make our efforts successful.* This important detail is huge because it reminds me that I need only to focus on making an effort and let God help with the actual success part.

I don't know about you, but I am often overwhelmed by the magnitude of all that I feel God has called me to do. When I begin to feel stressed and overwhelmed, it is because I have forgotten that wherever God guides, God provides.

It's not solely up to me to make myself successful. I must remember to lean fully on God for the success. I am responsible to put in the effort, and He will provide the success, in His perfect timing.

Are you feeling overwhelmed with something you know God has called you to do? Does the thought of actually accomplishing it seem unimaginable? Take a deep breath and relax.

Stop focusing on how you're going to make something successful. Instead, focus on putting in your best effort. Allow God to bring the success. Remember *God is God, and you're not*.

Today's Prayer:

Lord, thank you for Psalm 90:17. Thank you for reminding me that it is okay to pray for success. I pray that you will show me your approval and make my efforts successful. Whenever I begin to feel overwhelmed remind me that you're God and I'm not. I know that wherever you guide me you will provide the resources needed to fulfill your purpose. Remind me to focus on putting in my best effort and trust you will bring the success. In Jesus' name, I pray, AMEN.

DAY 26
WISDOM FOR FINDING REST

> *"Those who live in the shelter of the Most High*
>
> *will find rest in the shadow of the Almighty."*
>
> *Psalm 91:1 (NLT)*

FEELING POOPED OUT lately? Psalm 91:1 promises if we live in the shelter of our awesome heavenly Father, we WILL find rest!

You're probably thinking, well, that is great, but why don't I feel more rested then? I asked that same question.

This promise is for those who "live" in the shelter of the Most High, not for those who just visit on occasion or drive by, or use the drive-thru and get it *to go*, if you know what I mean.

Are you "living" in God's shelter? Have you decided to settle in? Have you put your clothes in the drawers, or are you still using a suitcase?

According to the dictionary, the word shelter means a place that provides food and protection. Interestingly, it doesn't mention this place is "temporary." Starting to see where I'm going with this?

God wants us to "live" in His shelter where He can provide for us and protect us. This place isn't so much a physical location where we need to be sitting with the Bible open all day long to experience the rest He's promising. It's more of a state of mind.

It's a state of knowing that no matter what is happening around me right now, God will provide for me and protect me and then acting accordingly. This mindset means, instead of acting fearful or constantly worrying about what's coming, remain confident, believing in God's promises in His Word.

Maintaining this state of mind is sometimes hard for me. I want to do a quick check-in in the morning and be on my merry way. But when I rush my morning time with Him, I quickly forget what He told me. That's if I even gave Him any time to speak in the first place. It's no wonder that by lunch time I'm back to my worried and restless state.

Instead of rushing your morning time with God, slow down and take your time. When I take the time to really dig into the Word and wait for what God wants to teach me, I'm filled with peace and rest.

Then, if I write down a verse that really spoke to me and look at it throughout the day, it's much easier to maintain that inner confidence in spite of my circumstances.

Life is not a sprint. It's a marathon. If you want to find rest, take the time to really live in the shelter of our Most High.

Today's Prayer:

Lord, I pray that you will help me to remember to really live in your shelter. Not rush through but take the time to dig into your Word every day. Remind me that when I feel restless and worried about the future, I'm forgetting your promise to provide for me and protect me. Lord, I want to feel your rest today. I'm fearful of (fill in the blank). I'm worried about (fill in the blank). I'm going to live in the shelter of you, my Most High, because that is where I will find rest, knowing that you will provide for and protect me no matter what the future holds. In Jesus' name, I pray, AMEN.

DAY 27
WISDOM FOR CONQUERING
NEGATIVE THOUGHTS

"If you make the Lord your refuge,

if you make the Most High your shelter,

no evil will conquer you,

no plague will come near your home."

Psalms 91:9-10 (NLT)

THE OTHER DAY I was battling some negative thoughts and feeling really discouraged. I just so happened to be reading Psalms 91:9-10 during my morning prayer time.

I immediately wrote the verse on an index card and kept it with me all day. Every time negative thoughts filled my mind, I pulled out the index card and started reading it over and over.

Reading and meditating on God's Word is the only thing that helps me conquer my negative thoughts and I know it will help you, too.

When you think negative thoughts, inevitably you

will start to feel discouraged. When you read God's Word and meditate on His promises, positive thoughts will soon replace your negative thoughts and peace will replace your discouragement.

For example; as I focus on God's promise in Psalms 91:9-10, that says *if I continually make God my refuge and shelter, He will not let evil conquer me*, even though my circumstance is the same on the outside, my heart will be at peace on the inside. Make sense?

I don't know what negative thoughts are discouraging you today. I do know that you can conquer those negative thoughts by meditating on God's promises like Psalms 91:9-10.

Today's Prayer:

Lord, in Psalms 91:9-10, you promise that if I come to you Lord, and make you my refuge and my shelter, no evil will conquer me, no plague will come near my home. Lord, I'm feeling discouraged by negative thoughts of (fill in the blank) so I come to you for refuge. I know that you will not let these evil thoughts conquer me. I am going to trust you and your promises from now on. I'm coming to you right now and ask you to replace the evil thoughts with your peace. I thank you for loving and protecting me. In Jesus' name, I pray, AMEN.

DAY 28
WISDOM FOR MULTIPLYING
MY FAITH

"Sing to the Lord. Bless his name!

Share the news of his saving work every single day!"

Psalm 96:2 (CEB)

WANT TO HAVE more faith? I have a tip that will radically multiply your faith. Are you ready? Listen closely because this is going to seem a bit too simple. You may laugh at first. But here you go:

Find a close group of friends with whom you can share what God is doing in your life. Share not only how He is blessing you but also how He is guiding, shaping, and correcting you.

So, how does this multiply your faith? Glad you asked! As soon as you start sharing how God is working in your life, others will naturally want to start sharing how He is working in their life, too.

Seeing God at work in other people's lives, not just your own, will explode your faith big time! Not only do you get to see God working in your life but also you see Him at work in their lives too. And, that's how you multiply your faith.

If you're not quite ready to share with a group of friends, start with one friend. Be open, honest, and real. Try to meet together weekly. Do a Bible study together or just meet for prayer. Before you know it, not only will your faith be growing and thriving but so will your friendships. That is just how our awesome God works.

Do what Psalm 96:2 says; *"…Share the news of his saving work every single day."* with a friend or a small group of girlfriends and watch your faith multiply. I dare you!

Today's Prayer:

Thank you Lord for all the amazing things you've done in my life. Help me to remember to share what you've done with others somehow every day. Give me the desire to be transparent and real with a couple of close friends, so we can grow in faith and in our friendships. Show me today who you want me to connect with. Help me to make this task a priority and use it to help grow my faith and friendships. In Jesus' name, I pray, AMEN.

DAY 29
WISDOM FOR WHEN
I'M DESPERATE

"He will listen to the prayers of the destitute.

He will not reject their pleas."

Psalm 102:17 (NLT)

HAVE YOU EVER been desperate for something? Have you ever wanted something so badly you found yourself on your knees begging God for it?

I have, many times. When I read this verse, I nearly fell over with excitement. Finally! A special verse just for us "beggars"!

If you're desperate for God to do something in your life, He promises in Psalm 102:17 to listen to the prayers of the destitute. He will not reject your pleas.

Here's my question for you. Are you pleading with God for anything? Have you gotten down on your knees and poured out your heart to Him lately? Or, are you busy trying to make that thing happen all on your own?

I did this one morning. I waited for everyone to

leave the house first, of course. Then I played a few of my favorite worship songs and spent some time pleading with God.

I poured out what was on my heart and then literally pleaded with Him for guidance, healing, and strength. Afterward, I felt the most amazing peace and joy ever.

If you're struggling with something in your life, when you have tired of trying to fix it on your own, do what I did. God will listen to your prayers. He will NOT reject your pleas.

Go to a quiet place alone where you can be real and raw with God and just pour out what's on your heart. Do it right now if you can. This is a short devotional, so you have no excuse.

If you want to feel God's presence like never before, now is the time. Don't put it off. How many times do I have to say it? God is waiting to listen to your prayers. HE WILL NOT REJECT YOUR PLEAS!

Today's Prayer:

Thank you Lord for your promise in Psalm 102:17! Thank you for promising to listen to the prayers of the destitute. Lord, I'm here in your presence right now, and I so need your help with (fill in the blank). I'm so done trying to fix it on my own. I am begging for your help. Thank you for not rejecting my pleas. In Jesus' name, I pray, AMEN.

DAY 30
WISDOM FOR OVERCOMING
NEGATIVE INFLUENCES

"Let all that I am praise the Lord;

may I never forget the good things he does for me."

Psalm 103:2 (NLT)

E VERY DAY, WE'RE beaten down by negative influences. See if the following scene sounds familiar to
you...

At work all day you endure *Negative Ned and Nancy*.
Back at home, you turn on the television to be immediately bombarded with how bad things are or will be very
soon.

If we turn off the television to get away from the negative vibes, our husband or children soon arrive bringing
plenty of depressing news in tow. If we eventually escape
to the bedroom to our cozy pillow-top thinking we'll
finally find reprieve in sleep, we're often awakened to
some horrible nightmare complete with real tears even.

Is this not what happens to you on a weekly basis?
The only difference for me is that I'm sometimes the one

full of negative news to report, which, for some reason, I decide to disseminate during mealtime. It's probably because I have somewhat of a captive audience.

In Psalm 103:2 David tells us first to praise the Lord with all that we are. Whether you're regularly beaten down by Negative Nancy or you're Negative Nancy herself, you'll find instant relief by praising the Lord. If you're struggling with what "praising the Lord" looks like, simply turn on your favorite worship song and sing along.

Second, David tells us never to forget the good things God does for us. Notice that this verse is not written in past tense. While writing down everything God has done for us in the past is great, it's important for us to acknowledge the things He is doing for us right now... today.

In case you're struggling with what those things might be, David cleverly provides a list in the next three verses. Psalms 103:3-5 (NLT) says; *"He forgives all my sins and heals all my diseases. He redeems me from death and crowns me with love and tender mercies. He fills my life with good things. My youth is renewed like the eagle's!"*

Verse three reminds us that God forgives all our sins and heals all our diseases. The sins He's talking about aren't the ones from way back when. These are the ones we're doing right now. I'd say that is a pretty good thing, wouldn't you?

Now it's your turn. Write down everything you can think of that God is doing for you right now. Use Psalms

103:3-5 as your guide. Write them down to help you remember throughout the day.

When you start to feel beaten down by all the negative influences, overcome them by letting all that you are praise the Lord and never forgetting the good things God is doing for you right now –today!

Today's Prayer:

Lord, thank you for reminding me to praise you and remember all the good things you are doing in my life. I praise you and thank you for (fill in the blank with your list). As I go about my day today, and negative influences threaten to beat me down, remind me of everything that you are doing for me right now. Please help me refuse to give in to the temptation to be negative myself. In Jesus' name, I pray, AMEN.

DAY 31
WISDOM FOR SHARING MY HOPE

"Has the Lord redeemed you? Then speak out!

Tell others he has redeemed you from your enemies."

Psalm 107:2 (NLT)

S OMETIMES I SHY away from sharing how God has helped me. I don't want to sound "preachy." I certainly don't want people to think I'm… you know…one of *those people*. They're weird.

Do you ever feel this way? Maybe that is exactly what Satan would want us to think.

With all the bad that is happening in the world today, maybe people are more hungry for hope than we think.

Psalm 107:2 is a call to share our hope of how God has redeemed us from our enemies. I'm not just talking about our physical enemies. I'm also talking about those invisible enemies you and I battle with every day like fear of rejection, depression, poor self-esteem, or habitual procrastination, for example.

Look, I'm no one special. I'm a high school dropout with attention deficit disorder (ADD). I have a terrible time staying focused on projects, let alone completing them.

So, when my first devotional book reached the "Amazon Best Seller" list, it was only because of God's amazing work, not mine. His miraculous power kept me focused just long enough to accomplish what He wanted to do.

God redeemed me from my enemy of distraction and lack of focus. What enemy has God redeemed you from? Has He redeemed you from doubt, depression, a failure, or a weakness? Have you told anyone?

You might think that what He's done in your life isn't news worthy. You're dead wrong!

Everyone is hungry for hope. Share yours with someone today!

Today's Prayer:

Lord, thank you for redeeming me from (fill in the blank). Thank you for reminding me to get out there and share what you've done in my life with others. I pray you will give me the courage to share my story, even if I'm afraid of what others might think of me. I pray you will use my story to encourage others and bring them closer to you. In Jesus' name, I pray, AMEN.

If you enjoyed this devotional book, please go to Amazon to leave a review. I would greatly appreciate it!

About the Author

Kristy Marcotte is a writer, speaker, and ministry leader. She is the founder of StraightTalkFor-Women.com where she helps women strengthen their faith, family, and friendships. Her blog posts, podcasts, and videos provide tips, tools, and God's truth for successful living. She and her husband have three adult daughters, two Miniature Schnauzers, and live in Kansas City, Missouri.

For more information on
how to connect with Kristy go to:
www.StraightTalkForWomen.com

Kristy's Story

Kristy accepted Christ as a child, but during her teen years stubbornly chose to do things "*her way*". Her poor choices resulted in dropping out of high school and pregnant by age twenty.

God's amazing power to turn mistakes into miracles and His sense of humor became evident when she discovered she was expecting TWINS!

Shortly after the twins' first birthday, Kristy and their father were married but hurt and resentment from their rocky start began to destroy the relationship. After being separated not once, but twice, both realized that serious help was needed if there was any chance of saving their marriage.

After several years of marriage counseling, completing a recovery program at their church, and large doses of prayer and determination, they gained a deeper faith and new tools to strengthen their marriage.

As a result of her personal trials, Kristy has become a passionate advocate for one of God's precious commitments – Marriage. Unfortunately, the U.S. continues to experience close to a 50% divorce rate annually.

Thankfully, Kristy and her husband did not become one of these statistics. With God's help, they have been married now for almost 25 years and share a much deeper commitment.

Besides being a wife and mom of three daughters; Kristy has also led a marriage support group sharing the tools she learned to help other wives strengthen their marriages.

Recently, Kristy's husband retired from serving 28 years in law enforcement. After having lived in Southern California since 1989 and calling Saddleback Church their home since 1992, they felt God calling them to move to the Midwest.

In spring of 2018, Kristy and her husband purchased property in the Kansas City area and are building their dream home.

Today, Kristy spends most days writing, speaking at women's events, and sharing tips, tools, and God's truth for successful living on her blog; StraightTalkFor-Women.com.

In her free time, Kristy can be found at various local sports parks watching her nieces' and nephews' games, or curled up on the couch with her husband and their two Miniature Schnauzers (Dexter and Oliver) watching a movie or Supercross, her favorite sport!

Acknowledgements

A huge thank you to Pat Casarez, Ernie Casarez, Mone Pace, Scott Pace, Linda Johnson, Mimi Kent, Rachel Moore, Debbie Nahodil, Kim Roberson, Jill Wilyard, Wendy Tran, Sharon Pease, and Celeste Herron for your amazing encouragement, guidance, wisdom, friendship, and constant prayer! A super huge thank you to my husband Brian for graciously allowing me to work all hours of the day and night to pursue my passion to write. Without you all, this book would not exist.

Resources for
When I Pray Volume 2

Free Journal Pages
Free Bible verse images
When I Pray Volume 2 Workbook

Other Books by Kristy

When I Pray
When I Pray Volume 3 – *coming soon*
When I Love – *coming soon*

Go to:
www.StraightTalkForWomen.com
for more information

www.ingramcontent.com/pod-product-compliance
Lightning Source LLC
Chambersburg PA
CBHW071619040426
42452CB00009B/1393